MW01133752

KNIT HATS
FOR BABIES

Let your playful side show when you're knitting cozy caps for the babies in your life! These precious designs reflect the fun of holidays and sports themes. Each can be made in three sizes, from newborn to 12 months.

LEISURE ARTS, INC. • Little Rock, Arkansas

FOOTBALL HAT

INTERMEDIATE

SHOPPING LIST

Yarn (Medium Weight)

[1.75 ounces, 80 yards
(50 grams, 73 meters) per skein]:

☐ Brown - 1{1-2} skein(s)
☐ White - small amount

Knitting Needles

Double pointed needles
(set of 5),

☐ Size 7 (4.5 mm)
or size needed for gauge

Additional Supplies

☐ Split-ring marker
☐ Yarn needle

SIZE INFORMATION

Newborn {3-6 months-12 months}
Finished Head Circumference:
12½{14¼-16}"/32{36-40.5} cm

Size Note: We have printed the
instructions for the sizes in different
colors to make it easier for you to find:

• Size Newborn in Blue
• Size 3-6 months in Pink
• Size 12 months in Green

Instructions in Black apply to all sizes.

GAUGE INFORMATION

In Stockinette Stitch,
   (knit every round)
   18 sts and 28 rnds = 4" (10 cm)

TECHNIQUE USED

K2 tog *(Fig. 5, page 27)*

INSTRUCTIONS
RIBBING

With Brown, cast on 56{64-72} sts.

Divide sts evenly onto 4 needles
*(see Using Double Pointed Knitting
Needles, page 26)*: 14{16-18} sts **each**
needle.

Place a split-ring marker around
the first stitch to indicate the
beginning of the round *(see Markers,
page 25)*.

Rnds 1-6 (Right side)**:** (K1, P1) around.

BODY

Knit 2{2-3} rnds.

Drop Brown; with White, knit
2{2-3} rnds.

Cut White.

With Brown, knit every rnd until
piece measures approximately
4{4½-5}"/10{11.5-12.5} cm from
cast on edge.

Drop Brown; with White, knit
2{2-3} rnds.

Cut White.

With Brown, knit one rnd.

SHAPING

Rnd 1: (K6, K2 tog) around:
49{56-63} sts.

Rnd 2: Knit around.

Rnd 3: (K5, K2 tog) around:
42{48-54} sts.

Rnd 4: Knit around.

Rnd 5: (K4, K2 tog) around:
35{40-45} sts.

Rnds 6 and 7: Knit around.

Rnd 8: (K3, K2 tog) around:
28{32-36} sts.

Rnds 9 and 10: Knit around.

Rnd 11: (K2, K2 tog) around: 21{24-27} sts.

Rnds 12 and 13: Knit around.

Rnd 14: (K1, K2 tog) around: 14{16-18} sts.

Rnd 15: K2 tog around: 7{8-9} sts.

Cut yarn leaving an 8" (20.5 cm) length for sewing. Thread yarn needle with end and slip remaining sts onto yarn needle; pull **tightly** to close and secure end.

LACING

Using photo as a guide for placement and Duplicate Stitch *(Figs. 9a & b, page 28)*, add White center line to center front of Hat beginning on third round above bottom White stripe and ending on third round below top White stripe. Add 4 White straight stitches *(Fig. 12, page 29)* evenly spaced on each side of center line.

BASEBALL HAT

■■□ **INTERMEDIATE**

SHOPPING LIST

Yarn (Medium Weight)

[1.75 ounces, 80 yards
(50 grams, 73 meters) per skein]:
☐ White - 1{1-2} skein(s)
☐ Red - small amount

Knitting Needles

Double pointed needles
(set of 5),
☐ Size 7 (4.5 mm)
or size needed for gauge

Additional Supplies

☐ Split-ring marker
☐ Yarn needle

SIZE INFORMATION

Newborn {3-6 months-12 months}
Finished Head Circumference:
12½{14¼-16}"/32{36-40.5} cm

Size Note: We have printed the
instructions for the sizes in different
colors to make it easier for you to find:
• Size Newborn in Blue
• Size 3-6 months in Pink
• Size 12 months in Green
Instructions in Black apply to all sizes.

GAUGE INFORMATION

In Stockinette Stitch,
 (knit every round)
 18 sts and 28 rnds = 4" (10 cm)

TECHNIQUE USED

🎥 K2 tog *(Fig. 5, page 27)*

INSTRUCTIONS
RIBBING

With White, cast on 56{64-72} sts.

🎥 Divide sts evenly onto 4 needles
*(see Using Double Pointed Knitting
Needles, page 26)*: 14{16-18} sts **each**
needle.

🎥 Place a split-ring marker around
the first stitch to indicate the
beginning of the round *(see Markers,
page 25)*.

Rnds 1 thru 6{6-8}: (K1, P1) around.

BODY

Knit every rnd until piece
measures approximately
4{4½-5}"/10{11.5-12.5} cm from
cast on edge.

SHAPING

Rnd 1: (K6, K2 tog) around:
49{56-63} sts.

Rnd 2: Knit around.

Rnd 3: (K5, K2 tog) around:
42{48-54} sts.

Rnd 4: Knit around.

Rnd 5: (K4, K2 tog) around:
35{40-45} sts.

Rnd 6: Knit around.

Rnd 7: (K3, K2 tog) around:
28{32-36} sts.

Rnd 8: Knit around.

Rnd 9: (K2, K2 tog) around:
21{24-27} sts.

Rnd 10: Knit around.

Rnd 11: (K1, K2 tog) around:
14{16-18} sts.

Rnd 12: K2 tog around: 7{8-9} sts.

Cut yarn leaving an 8" (20.5 cm) length for sewing. 📹 Thread yarn needle with end and slip remaining sts onto yarn needle; pull **tightly** to close and secure end.

STITCHING

Using photo as a guide for placement and 📹 Duplicate Stitch *(Figs. 9a & b, page 28)*, add 4 Red lines for "stitching lines" spaced equally around.

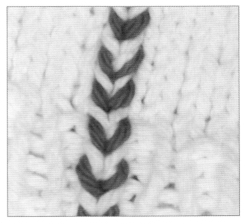

BASKETBALL HAT

■■■□ INTERMEDIATE

SHOPPING LIST

Yarn (Medium Weight)
[5 ounces, 256 yards
(141 grams, 234 meters)
per skein]:
- ☐ Brown - 1 skein
- ☐ Black - small amount

Knitting Needles
Double pointed needles
(set of 5),
- ☐ Size 7 (4.5 mm)
  or size needed for gauge

Additional Supplies
- ☐ Split-ring marker
- ☐ Yarn needle

SIZE INFORMATION
Newborn {3-6 months-12 months}
Finished Head Circumference:
12½{14¼-16}"/32{36-40.5} cm

Size Note: We have printed the
instructions for the sizes in different
colors to make it easier for you to find:
- Size Newborn in Blue
- Size 3-6 months in Pink
- Size 12 months in Green

Instructions in Black apply to all sizes.

GAUGE INFORMATION
In Stockinette Stitch,
   (knit every round)
   18 sts and 28 rnds = 4" (10 cm)

TECHNIQUE USED
📹 K2 tog (*Fig. 5, page 27*)

INSTRUCTIONS
BODY
With Brown, cast on 56{64-72} sts.

📹 Divide sts evenly onto 4 needles
(*see Using Double Pointed Knitting
Needles, page 26*): 14{16-18} sts **each**
needle.

📹 Place a split-ring marker around
the first stitch to indicate the
beginning of the round (*see Markers,
page 25*).

Knit every rnd until piece
measures approximately
5{5½-6}"/12.5{14-15} cm from
cast on edge.

SHAPING
Rnd 1: (K6, K2 tog) around:
49{56-63} sts.

Rnd 2: Knit around.

Rnd 3: (K5, K2 tog) around:
42{48-54} sts.

Rnd 4: Knit around.

Rnd 5: (K4, K2 tog) around:
35{40-45} sts.

Rnd 6: Knit around.

Rnd 7: (K3, K2 tog) around:
28{32-36} sts.

Rnd 8: Knit around.

Rnd 9: (K2, K2 tog) around:
21{24-27} sts.

Rnd 10: Knit around.

Rnd 11: (K1, K2 tog) around:
14{16-18} sts.

Rnd 12: K2 tog around: 7{8-9} sts.

Cut yarn leaving an 8" (20.5 cm)
length for sewing. 📹 Thread yarn
needle with end and slip remaining
sts onto yarn needle; pull **tightly** to
close and secure end.

LINES

Using Diagram as a guide for placement and 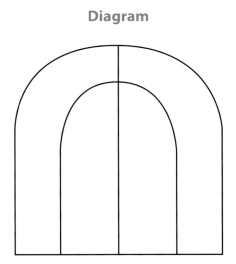 backstitch *(Fig. 11, page 29)*, add Black lines.
Weave in yarn ends making sure they don't show when bottom edge is rolled up.

Diagram

CHRISTMAS HAT

 **INTERMEDIATE**

SHOPPING LIST

Yarn (Medium Weight)
[3.5 ounces, 170 yards
(100 grams, 156 meters)
per skein]:
☐ Red - 1 skein

Long eyelash (Bulky Weight) 🟦5
[1.75 ounces, 64 yards
(50 grams, 58 meters) per skein]:
☐ White - 1 skein

Knitting Needles
Double pointed needles
(set of 5),
☐ Size 7 (4.5 mm)
or size needed for gauge

Additional Supplies
☐ Split-ring marker
☐ Yarn needle

SIZE INFORMATION

Newborn {3-6 months-12 months}
Finished Head Circumference:
12½{14¼-16}"/32{36-40.5} cm

Size Note: We have printed the
instructions for the sizes in different
colors to make it easier for you to find:
• Size Newborn in Blue
• Size 3-6 months in Pink
• Size 12 months in Green
Instructions in Black apply to all sizes.

GAUGE INFORMATION

In Stockinette Stitch,
    (knit every round)
    18 sts and 28 rnds = 4" (10 cm)

TECHNIQUES USED

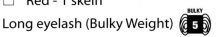 Purl increase *(Fig. 4, page 27)*
🎥 K2 tog *(Fig. 5, page 27)*
🎥 P2 tog *(Fig. 7, page 28)*

INSTRUCTIONS
BODY

With White, cast on 56{64-72} sts.

🎥 Divide sts evenly onto 4 needles
*(see Using Double Pointed Knitting
Needles, page 26)*: 14{16-18} sts **each**
needle.

🎥 Place a split-ring marker around
the first stitch to indicate the
beginning of the round *(see Markers,
page 25)*.

Rnds 1 thru 14{16-18} (Right side):
Knit around.

Cut White.

With Red, knit every rnd until
piece measures approximately
5{5½-6}"/12.5{14-15} cm from
cast on edge.

SHAPING

Rnd 1: (K6, K2 tog) around: 49{56-63} sts.

Rnd 2: Knit around.

Rnd 3: (K5, K2 tog) around: 42{48-54} sts.

Rnd 4: Knit around.

Rnd 5: (K4, K2 tog) around: 35{40-45} sts.

Rnds 6-9: Knit around.

Rnd 10: (K3, K2 tog) around: 28{32-36} sts.

Rnds 11-18: Knit around.

Rnd 19: (K2, K2 tog) around: 21{24-27} sts.

Rnds 20-28: Knit around.

Rnd 29: (K1, K2 tog) around: 14{16-18} sts.

Rnds 30-38: Knit around.

Rnd 39: K2 tog around: 7{8-9} sts.

Rnds 40-50: Knit around.

Rnd 51: K1{0-1} *(see Zeros, page 26)*, K2 tog around; slip remaining sts onto one double pointed needle: 4{4-5} sts.

KNITTED CORD

Row 1: Knit across, do **not** turn; slide sts to opposite end of needle.

Repeat Row 1 until Knitted Cord measures approximately 1" (2.5 cm).

Cut yarn leaving an 8" (20.5 cm) length for sewing. Thread yarn needle with end and slip remaining sts onto yarn needle; pull **tightly** to close and secure end.

POM-POM

With White, cast on 8 sts leaving a long end for sewing and attaching.

Divide sts evenly onto 4 needles.

Place a split-ring marker around the first stitch to indicate the beginning of the round.

Rnd 1: Purl around.

Rnd 2: Purl increase in each st around: 16 sts.

Rnds 3-6: Purl around.

Rnd 7: P2 tog around: 8 sts.

Cut yarn leaving an 8" (20.5 cm) length for sewing. Thread yarn needle with end and slip remaining sts onto yarn needle; pull **tightly** to close and secure end.

Stuff pom-pom with White yarn. Thread yarn needle with long end and weave through cast on sts; pull **tightly** to close and secure end. With same yarn, attach pom-pom to top of Hat.

EASTER HAT

Shown on page 12.

SHOPPING LIST

Yarn (Medium Weight)

[5 ounces, 256 yards
(141 grams, 234 meters)
per skein]:
- ☐ Purple - 1 skein
- ☐ Pink - small amount
- ☐ Blue - small amount
- ☐ Yellow - small amount

[4 ounces, 204 yards
(113 grams, 187 meters)
per skein]:
- ☐ Variegated - 15 yards
  (13.5 meters)

Knitting Needles
Double pointed needles
(set of 5),
- ☐ Size 7 (4.5 mm)
  or size needed for gauge

Crochet Hook
- ☐ Size F (3.75 mm)
  (for fringe only)

Additional Supplies
- ☐ Split-ring marker
- ☐ Yarn needle

SIZE INFORMATION

Newborn {3-6 months-12 months}
Finished Head Circumference:
12½{14¼-16}"/32{36-40.5} cm

Size Note: We have printed the
instructions for the sizes in different
colors to make it easier for you to find:
- Size Newborn in Blue
- Size 3-6 months in Pink
- Size 12 months in Green

Instructions in Black apply to all sizes.

GAUGE INFORMATION

In Stockinette Stitch,
(knit every round)
18 sts and 28 rnds = 4" (10 cm)

TECHNIQUE USED

🎥 K2 tog *(Fig. 5, page 27)*

INSTRUCTIONS
BODY

With Variegated, cast on 56{64-72} sts.

🎥 Divide sts evenly onto 4 needles
*(see Using Double Pointed Knitting
Needles, page 26)*: 14{16-18} sts **each**
needle.

🎥 Place a split-ring marker around
the first stitch to indicate the
beginning of the round *(see Markers,
page 25)*.

Rnds 1 thru 8{8-10}: Knit around.

Cut Variegated.

With Purple, knit every rnd until
piece measures approximately
5{5½-6}"/12.5{14-15} cm from
cast on edge.

SHAPING

Rnd 1: (K6, K2 tog) around:
49{56-63} sts.

Rnd 2: Knit around.

Rnd 3: (K5, K2 tog) around:
42{48-54} sts.

Rnd 4: Knit around.

Rnd 5: (K4, K2 tog) around:
35{40-45} sts.

Rnds 6-9: Knit around.

Rnd 10: (K3, K2 tog) around:
28{32-36} sts.

Repeat Row 1 until Knitted Cord measures approximately 1" (2.5 cm).

Cut yarn leaving an 8" (20.5 cm) length for sewing.

Cut 8{8-10} strands of Variegated each 8" (20.5 cm) long.
Hold 2 strands of yarn together and fold in half. Insert hook in first st on needle, pull folded end of yarn through st and draw loose ends through folded end; do **not** remove the st from the needle. Repeat with remaining sts.

📹 Thread yarn needle with long end and weave through sts on the needle; pull **tightly** to close and secure end.

Using photo as a guide, work 📹 French knots (wrapping 5 times) *(Fig. 13, page 29)*, using Pink, Blue, and Yellow and spacing randomly on Hat.

Rnds 11-18: Knit around.

Rnd 19: (K2, K2 tog) around: 21{24-27} sts.

Rnds 20-28: Knit around.

Rnd 29: (K1, K2 tog) around: 14{16-18} sts.

Rnds 30-38: Knit around.

Rnd 39: K2 tog around: 7{8-9} sts.

Rnds 40-50: Knit around.

Rnd 51: K1{0-1} *(see Zeros, page 26)*, K2 tog around; slip remaining sts onto one double pointed needle: 4{4-5} sts.

KNITTED CORD
Row 1: Knit across, do **not** turn; slide sts to opposite end of needle.

ST. PATRICK'S DAY HAT

Shown on page 15.

 **INTERMEDIATE**

SHOPPING LIST

Yarn (Medium Weight) **MEDIUM 4**

[3.5 ounces, 205 yards
(100 grams, 187 meters)
per skein]:

☐ Green - 1 skein

☐ Dk Green - small amount

Knitting Needles

Double pointed needles
(set of 5),

☐ Size 7 (4.5 mm)

or size needed for gauge

Straight needles,
(for Shamrock only)

☐ Size 4 (3.5 mm)

Crochet Hook

☐ Size D (3.25 mm)
(for Stem only)

Additional Supplies

☐ Split-ring marker

☐ Yarn needle

SIZE INFORMATION

Newborn {3-6 months-12 months}

Finished Head Circumference:

12½{14¼-16}"/32{36-40.5} cm

Size Note: We have printed the
instructions for the sizes in different
colors to make it easier for you to find:

• Size Newborn in Blue

• Size 3-6 months in Pink

• Size 12 months in Green

Instructions in Black apply to all sizes.

GAUGE INFORMATION

With larger size knitting needles,
   in Stockinette Stitch,
   (knit every round)
   18 sts and 28 rnds = 4" (10 cm)

TECHNIQUES USED

Knit increase *(Figs. 3a & b,
   page 27)*

K2 tog *(Fig. 5, page 27)*

INSTRUCTIONS
BODY

With Green and using larger size
knitting needles, cast on 56{64-72} sts.

Divide sts evenly onto 4 needles
*(see Using Double Pointed Knitting
Needles, page 26)*: 14{16-18} sts **each**
needle.

Place a split-ring marker around
the first stitch to indicate the
beginning of the round *(see Markers,
page 25)*.

Knit every rnd until piece
measures approximately
5{5½-6}"/12.5{14-15} cm from
cast on edge.

SHAPING

Rnd 1 (Right side)**:** (K6, K2 tog)
around: 49{56-63} sts.

Rnd 2: Knit around.

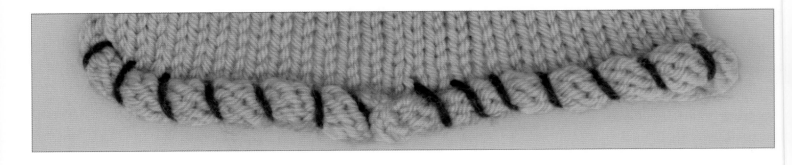

Rnd 3: (K5, K2 tog) around: 42{48-54} sts.

Rnd 4: Knit around.

Rnd 5: (K4, K2 tog) around: 35{40-45} sts.

Rnds 6-8: Knit around.

Rnd 9: (K3, K2 tog) around: 28{32-36} sts.

Rnds 10-12: Knit around.

Rnd 13: (K2, K2 tog) around: 21{24-27} sts.

Rnds 14-16: Knit around.

Rnd 17: (K1, K2 tog) around: 14{16-18} sts.

Rnds 18-20: Knit around.

Rnd 21: K2 tog around: 7{8-9} sts.

Rnds 22-24: Knit around.

Rnd 25: K1{0-1} *(see Zeros, page 26)*, K2 tog around; slip remaining sts onto one double pointed needle: 4{4-5} sts.

KNITTED CORD
Row 1: Knit across, do **not** turn; slide sts to opposite end of needle.

Repeat Row 1 until Knitted Cord measures approximately 3" (7.5 cm).

Cut yarn leaving an 8" (20.5 cm) length for sewing. 📷 Thread yarn needle with end and slip remaining sts onto yarn needle; pull **tightly** to close and secure end.

SHAMROCK

LEAF (Make 3)
With Dk Green, using smaller size needles and leaving a long end for sewing, cast on 2 sts.

Row 1 (Right side)**:** Knit increase in each st across: 4 sts.

Row 2: Knit across.

Rows 3 and 4: Knit increase in each st across: 16 sts.

Bind off all sts in **knit**.
Thread yarn needle with long end from cast on edge and sew ends of rows together to form a circle; secure end, do **not** cut yarn.

Thread yarn needle with long end of one Leaf. With **wrong** sides together, sew two Leaves together, using 3 sts; secure end. Thread yarn needle with long end of remaining Leaf. With **wrong** sides together, sew remaining Leaf to joined Leaves, using 3 sts; do **not** cut yarn.
Sew center together and secure end.

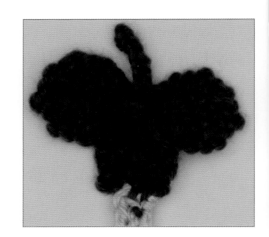

🎥 *See Basic Crochet Stitches, page 30.*

Stem: With crochet hook, join Dk Green with slip st to center of Shamrock; ch 7, slip st in back ridge of second ch from hook and each ch across, slip st in same sp as joining; finish off.

Using photo as a guide for placement, sew center Leaf of Shamrock to top of Knitted Cord.

Allow bottom edge of Hat to roll to the **right** side. Thread yarn needle with Dk Green. Using photo as a guide for placement on page 14, with bottom edge toward you, and

working from **right** to **left**, insert needle from **wrong** side into center of a st above the roll and pull through, ★ bring needle to the **wrong** side, skip next st and insert needle into center of next st above the roll and pull through **loosely**; repeat from ★ around.

HEART HAT

 ◼◼◼◻ INTERMEDIATE

SHOPPING LIST

Yarn (Medium Weight) [4]

[3.5 ounces, 207 yards (100 grams, 188 meters) per skein]:

- ☐ White - 1 skein
- ☐ Red - 1 skein

Knitting Needles

Straight needles,

- ☐ Size 7 (4.5 mm)
  or size needed for gauge
- ☐ Size 3 (3.25 mm)
  (for Heart only)

Crochet Hook

- ☐ Size D (3.25 mm)
  (for String only)

Additional Supplies

- ☐ Stitch holder
- ☐ Yarn needle
- ☐ Polyester fiberfill

SIZE INFORMATION

Newborn {3-6 months-12 months}

Finished Head Circumference:

12½{14¼-16}"/32{36-40.5} cm

Size Note: We have printed the instructions for the sizes in different colors to make it easier for you to find:

- Size Newborn in Blue
- Size 3-6 months in Pink
- Size 12 months in Green

Instructions in Black apply to all sizes.

GAUGE INFORMATION

With larger size knitting needles,
  in Stockinette Stitch,
  (knit one row, purl one row)
  18 sts and 28 rows = 4" (10 cm)

TECHNIQUES USED

- 🎥 Knit increase (*Figs. 3a & b, page 27*)
- 🎥 K2 tog (*Fig. 5, page 27*)
- 🎥 SSK (*Figs. 6a-c, page 27*)
- 🎥 P2 tog (*Fig. 7, page 28*)
- 🎥 Slip 1 as if to **purl**, P2 tog, PSSO (*Figs. 8a & b, page 28*)

INSTRUCTIONS
FRONT BOTTOM RIBBING

With Red and using larger size knitting needles, cast on 30{34-38} sts.

Rows 1-5: (K1, P1) across.

Cut Red.

Row 6 (Right side)**:** With White, knit across.

BODY

Beginning with a **purl** row, work in Stockinette Stitch until piece measures approximately 9½{11½-13½}"/24{29-34.5} cm from cast on edge, ending by working a **purl** row.

Cut White.

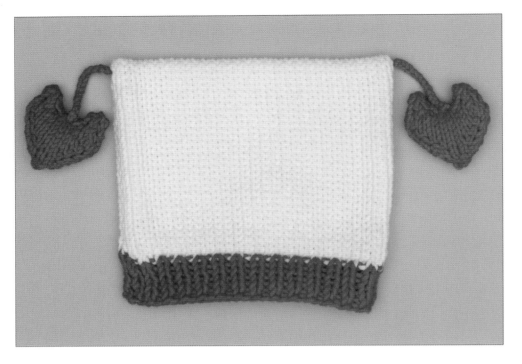

BACK BOTTOM RIBBING

Row 1: With Red, knit across.

Rows 2-6: (K1, P1) across.

Bind off all sts **loosely** in ribbing.

With **right** sides facing, fold piece in half matching ribbing. 📹 Weave side seams *(Fig. 10, page 29)*.

HEART (Make 2)
HALF (Make 2)

With Red, using smaller size knitting needles and leaving a long end for sewing on one Half only, cast on 3 sts.

Row 1: Purl across.

Row 2 (Right side)**:** Knit increase in next st, K1, knit increase in last st: 5 sts.

Row 3: Purl across.

Row 4: K1, (knit increase in next st, K1) twice: 7 sts.

Row 5: Purl across.

Row 6: K1, knit increase in next st, K3, knit increase in next st, K1: 9 sts.

Row 7: Purl across.

Row 8: K1, knit increase in next st, K5, knit increase in next st, K1: 11 sts.

Row 9: Purl across.

Row 10: K1, knit increase in next st, K7, knit increase in next st, K1: 13 sts.

Row 11: P5, P2 tog, P6: 12 sts.

First Side

Row 1: K1, SSK, K1, K2 tog, slip remaining 6 sts onto st holder: 4 sts.

Row 2: P1, P2 tog, P1: 3 sts.

Row 3: Knit across.

Row 4: Slip 1 as if to **purl**, P2 tog, PSSO: one st.

Cut yarn, pull end through last st.

Second Side

Row 1: Slip 6 sts from st holder onto smaller size knitting needle, K1, SSK, K1, K2 tog: 4 sts.

Complete same as First Side.

With **wrong** sides of two Halves together, sew pieces together stuffing lightly with fiberfill **before** closing.

STRING

📹 *See Basic Crochet Stitches, page 30.*

Using crochet hook, join Red with slip st in center top indent of Heart; ch 10; finish off leaving a long end for sewing.

Thread yarn needle with long end and attach Heart to one top corner of Hat.

GHOST HAT

Shown on page 21.

 INTERMEDIATE

SHOPPING LIST

Yarn (Medium Weight)
[1.75 ounces, 80 yards
(50 grams, 73 meters) per skein]:
☐ White - 1{1-2} skein(s)
[2 ounces, 99 yards
(57 grams, 90 meters) per skein]:
☐ Black - small amount

Knitting Needles

Double pointed needles
(set of 5),
☐ Size 7 (4.5 mm)
or size needed for gauge
Straight needles (for Eyes only),
☐ Size 6 (4 mm)

Additional Supplies

☐ Split-ring marker
☐ Yarn needle

SIZE INFORMATION

Newborn {3-6 months-12 months}
Finished Head Circumference:
12½{14¼-16}"/32{36-40.5} cm

Size Note: We have printed the
instructions for the sizes in different
colors to make it easier for you to find:
• Size Newborn in Blue
• Size 3-6 months in Pink
• Size 12 months in Green
Instructions in Black apply to all sizes.

GAUGE INFORMATION

With larger size knitting needles,
in Stockinette Stitch,
(knit every round)
18 sts and 28 rnds = 4" (10 cm)

TECHNIQUES USED

Knit increase *(Figs. 3a & b,
page 27)*
K2 tog *(Fig. 5, page 27)*

INSTRUCTIONS
BODY

With White and using larger size
knitting needles, cast on 56{64-72} sts.

Divide sts evenly onto 4 needles
*(see Using Double Pointed Knitting
Needles, page 26)*: 14{16-18} sts each
needle.

Place a split-ring marker around
the first stitch to indicate the
beginning of the round *(see Markers,
page 25)*.

Knit every rnd until piece
measures approximately
5{5½-6}"/12.5{14-15} cm from
cast on edge.

SHAPING

Rnd 1: (K6, K2 tog) around:
49{56-63} sts.

Rnd 2: Knit around.

Cut yarn leaving an 8" (20.5 cm) length for sewing. 🎥 Thread yarn needle with end and slip remaining sts onto yarn needle; pull **tightly** to close and secure end.

Tie Knitted Cord in a knot.

EYE (Make 2)
With Black, using smaller size knitting needles and leaving a long end for sewing, cast on 3 sts.

Rows 1 and 2: Knit increase in each st across: 12 sts.

Row 3: (K1, knit increase in next st) across: 18 sts.

Row 4: Knit across.

Bind off all sts in **knit**.

Thread yarn needle with long end from cast on edge and sew ends of rows together to form a circle.

Using photo as a guide for placement, sew Eyes to front of Hat, spacing them four stitches apart.

Using photo as a guide for placement and 🎥 backstitch (*Fig. 11, page 29*), add Black mouth across 14 stitches centered under the Eyes. Add Black 🎥 straight stitch lines to mouth (*Fig. 12, page 29*).

Rnd 3: (K5, K2 tog) around: 42{48-54} sts.

Rnd 4: Knit around.

Rnd 5: (K4, K2 tog) around: 35{40-45} sts.

Rnd 6: Knit around.

Rnd 7: (K3, K2 tog) around: 28{32-36} sts.

Rnd 8: Knit around.

Rnd 9: (K2, K2 tog) around: 21{24-27} sts.

Rnd 10: Knit around.

Rnd 11: (K1, K2 tog) around: 14{16-18} sts.

Rnd 12: K2 tog around: 7{8-9} sts.

Rnd 13: K1{0-1} (*see Zeros, page 26*), K2 tog around; slip remaining sts onto one double pointed needle: 4{4-5} sts.

KNITTED CORD
Row 1: Knit across, do **not** turn; slide sts to opposite end of needle.

Repeat Row 1 until Knitted Cord measures approximately 5" (12.5 cm).

WITCH HAT

 **INTERMEDIATE**

SHOPPING LIST

Yarn (Medium Weight) 🪢 **MEDIUM 4**
[3.5 ounces, 146 yards
(100 grams, 134 meters)
per skein]:
☐ Black - 1{1-2} skein(s)
☐ Orange - 15 yards
   (13.5 meters)

Knitting Needles
Double pointed needles
(set of 5),
☐ Size 6 (4 cm) **and**
☐ Size 7 (4.5 mm)
   or sizes needed for gauge

Additional Supplies
☐ Split-ring marker
☐ Yarn needle

SIZE INFORMATION
Newborn {3-6 months-12 months}
Finished Head Circumference:
12½{14-16}"/32{35.5-40.5} cm

Size Note: We have printed the
instructions for the sizes in different
colors to make it easier for you to find:
• Size Newborn in Blue
• Size 3-6 months in Pink
• Size 12 months in Green
Instructions in Black apply to all sizes.

GAUGE INFORMATION
With larger size knitting needles ,
   in Stockinette Stitch,
   (knit every round)
   18 sts and 28 rnds = 4" (10 cm)

TECHNIQUES USED
📹 Knit increase (*Figs. 3a & b,*
   page 27)
📹 K2 tog (*Fig. 5, page 27*)

INSTRUCTIONS
BODY
With Black and using larger size
knitting needles, cast on 56{64-72} sts.

📹 Divide sts evenly onto 4 needles
(*see Using Double Pointed Knitting
Needles, page 26*): 14{16-18} sts **each**
needle.

📹 Place a split-ring marker around
the first stitch to indicate the
beginning of the round (*see Markers,
page 25*).

Knit every rnd until piece
measures approximately
5{5½-6}"/12.5{14-15} cm from
cast on edge.

SHAPING
Rnd 1 (Right side)**:** (K6, K2 tog)
around: 49{56-63} sts.

Rnd 2: Knit around.

Rnd 3: (K5, K2 tog) around:
42{48-54} sts.

Rnd 4: Knit around.

Rnd 5: (K4, K2 tog) around:
35{40-45} sts.

Rnds 6-11: Knit around.

Rnd 12: (K3, K2 tog) around: 28{32-36} sts.

Rnds 13-18: Knit around.

Rnd 19: (K2, K2 tog) around: 21{24-27} sts.

Rnds 20-25: Knit around.

Rnd 26: (K1, K2 tog) around: 14{16-18} sts.

Rnds 27-32: Knit around.

Rnd 33: K2 tog around: 7{8-9} sts.

Rnds 34-39: Knit around.

Rnd 40: K1{0-1} *(see Zeros, page 26)*, K2 tog around: 4{4-5} sts.

Rnds 41-44: Knit around.

Cut yarn leaving an 8" (20.5 cm) length for sewing. Thread yarn needle with end and slip remaining sts onto yarn needle; pull **tightly** to close and secure end.

BRIM

With **right** side of Hat facing, using smaller size knitting needles, and Black, pick up 56{64-72} sts one rnd **below** cast on edge *(Fig. 1)*: 56{64-72} sts.

Fig. 1

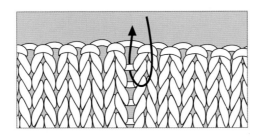

Rnd 1: Knit around.

Rnd 2: Purl around.

Rnd 3: (K1, knit increase in next st) around: 84{96-108} sts.

Change to larger size knitting needles.

Rnd 4: Purl around.

Rnd 5: Knit around.

Rnd 6: Purl around.

Rnd 7: (K3, knit increase in next st) around: 105{120-135} sts.

Rnds 8-12: Repeat Rows 4 and 5 twice, then repeat Row 4 once **more**.

Using smaller size knitting needle, bind off all sts in **knit**.

BAND

With Orange and using smaller size knitting needles, cast on 5 sts.

Row 1: Knit across.

Repeat Row 1 until Band fits around the Hat above Brim.

Bind off all sts in **knit**, leaving a long end for sewing.

Thread yarn needle with long end. Sew cast on edge and bind off edge together.

Place Band on Hat above the Brim and tack in place.

GENERAL INSTRUCTIONS

ABBREVIATIONS

ch	chain(s)
cm	centimeters
K	knit
mm	millimeters
P	purl
PSSO	pass slipped stitch over
Rnd(s)	Round(s)
SSK	slip, slip, knit
st(s)	stitch(es)
tog	together
YO	yarn over

SYMBOLS & TERMS

( ) or [ ] — work enclosed instructions **as many** times as specified by the number immediately following **or** contains explanatory remarks.

colon (:) — the number(s) given after a colon at the end of a row or round denote(s) the number of stitches you should have on that row or round.

GAUGE

Exact gauge is **essential** for proper size. Before beginning your Hat, make a sample swatch in the yarn and needles specified in the individual instructions. After completing the swatch, measure it, counting your stitches and rows/rounds carefully. If your swatch is larger or smaller than specified, **make another, changing needle size to get the correct gauge**. Keep trying until you find the size needles that will give you the specified gauge.

MARKERS

When using double pointed needles, a split-ring marker is placed around the first stitch of the round to indicate the beginning of a round. Place a marker as instructed and move it up at the beginning of each round.

KNIT TERMINOLOGY	
UNITED STATES	**INTERNATIONAL**
gauge =	tension
bind off =	cast off
yarn over (YO) =	yarn forward (yfwd) **or** yarn around needle (yrn)

Yarn Weight Symbol & Names	LACE 0	SUPER FINE 1	FINE 2	LIGHT 3	MEDIUM 4	BULKY 5	SUPER BULKY 6
Type of Yarns in Category	Fingering, size 10 crochet thread	Sock, Fingering, Baby	Sport, Baby	DK, Light Worsted	Worsted, Afghan, Aran	Chunky, Craft, Rug	Bulky, Roving
Knit Gauge Range* in Stockinette St to 4" (10 cm)	33-40** sts	27-32 sts	23-26 sts	21-24 sts	16-20 sts	12-15 sts	6-11 sts
Advised Needle Size Range	000-1	1 to 3	3 to 5	5 to 7	7 to 9	9 to 11	11 and larger

*GUIDELINES ONLY: The chart above reflects the most commonly used gauges and needle sizes for specific yarn categories.

** Lace weight yarns are usually knitted on larger needles to create lacy openwork patterns. Accordingly, a gauge range is difficult to determine. Always follow the gauge stated in your pattern.

ZEROS

To consolidate the length of an involved pattern, zeros are sometimes used so that all sizes can be combined. For example, K1{0-1} means sizes Newborn and 12 months would K1 and size 3-6 months would do nothing.

USING DOUBLE POINTED KNITTING NEEDLES

When working a piece that is too small to use a circular knitting needle, double pointed knitting needles are required. Divide the stitches into fourths and slip one-fourth of the stitches onto each of 4 double pointed needles *(Fig. 2a)*, forming a square *(Fig. 2b)*. Do **not** twist the cast on ridge. With the fifth needle, knit across the stitches on the first needle. You will now have an empty needle with which to knit the stitches from the next needle. Work the first stitch of each needle firmly to prevent gaps. Continue working around without turning the work.

KNITTING NEEDLES		
UNITED STATES	ENGLISH U.K.	METRIC (mm)
0	13	2
1	12	2.25
2	11	2.75
3	10	3.25
4	9	3.5
5	8	3.75
6	7	4
7	6	4.5
8	5	5
9	4	5.5
10	3	6
10½	2	6.5
11	1	8
13	00	9
15	000	10
17	---	12.75
19	---	15
35	---	19
50	---	25

Fig. 2a

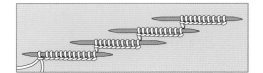

Fig. 2b

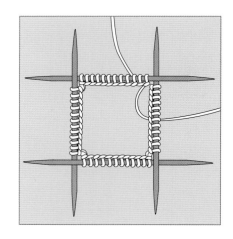

◖□□□ **BEGINNER**	Projects for first-time knitters using basic knit and purl stitches. Minimal shaping.
◖■□□ **EASY**	Projects using basic stitches, repetitive stitch patterns, simple color changes, and simple shaping and finishing.
◖■■□ **INTERMEDIATE**	Projects with a variety of stitches, such as basic cables and lace, simple intarsia, double-pointed needles and knitting in the round needle techniques, mid-level shaping and finishing.
◖■■■ **EXPERIENCED**	Projects using advanced techniques and stitches, such as short rows, fair isle, more intricate intarsia, cables, lace patterns, and numerous color changes.

INCREASES
KNIT INCREASE

Knit the next stitch but do **not** slip the old stitch off the left needle *(Fig. 3a)*. Insert the right needle into the **back** loop of the **same** stitch and knit it *(Fig. 3b)*, then slip the old stitch off the left needle.

Fig. 3a

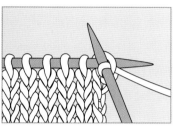

Fig. 3b

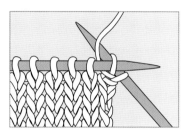

PURL INCREASE

Purl the next stitch but do **not** slip the old stitch off the left needle. Insert the right needle into the **back** loop of the **same** stitch *(Fig. 4)* and purl it, then slip the old stitch off the left needle.

Fig. 4

DECREASES
KNIT 2 TOGETHER *(abbreviated K2 tog)*

Insert the right needle into the **front** of the first two stitches on the left needle as if to **knit** *(Fig. 5)*, then **knit** them together as if they were one stitch.

Fig. 5

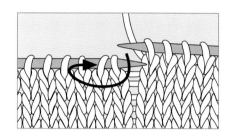

SLIP, SLIP, KNIT *(abbreviated SSK)*

Separately slip two stitches as if to **knit** *(Fig. 6a)*. Insert the left needle into the **front** of both slipped stitches *(Fig. 6b)* and then **knit** them together as if they were one stitch *(Fig. 6c)*.

Fig. 6a

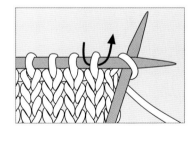

Fig. 6b

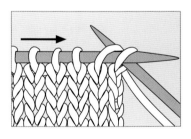

Fig. 6c

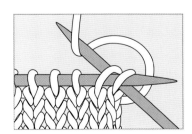

PURL 2 TOGETHER *(abbreviated P2 tog)*

Insert the right needle into the **front** of the first two stitches on the left needle as if to **purl** *(Fig. 7)*, then **purl** them together as if they were one stitch.

Fig. 7

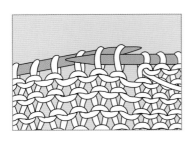

SLIP 1, PURL 2 TOGETHER, PASS SLIPPED STITCH OVER *(abbreviated slip 1, P2 tog, PSSO)*

Slip one stitch as if to **purl** *(Fig. 8a)*, then purl the next two stitches together *(Fig. 7)*. With the left needle, bring the slipped stitch over the stitch just made *(Fig. 8b)* and off the needle.

Fig. 8a   **Fig. 8b**

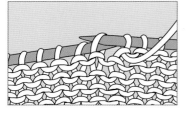 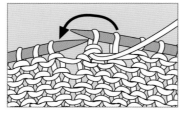

DUPLICATE STITCH

Duplicate Stitch is worked on Stockinette Stitch. Each knit stitch forms a V and you want to completely cover that V, so that the design appears to have been knit into the Hat. Thread a yarn needle with an 18" (45.5 cm) length of yarn. Beginning at the bottom of the design and with **right** side facing, bring the needle up from the **wrong** side at the base of the V, leaving an end to be woven in later (never tie knots). The needle should always go between the strands of yarn. Follow the right side of the V up and insert the needle from **right** to **left** under the legs of the V immediately above it, keeping the yarn on top of the stitch *(Fig. 9a)*, and draw through. Follow the left side of the V back down to the base and insert the needle back through the bottom of the same stitch where the first stitch began *(Fig. 9b, Duplicate Stitch completed)*.

Repeat for each stitch, keeping tension even with tension of knit fabric to avoid puckering.

When a length of yarn is finished, run it under several stitches on back of work to secure.

Fig. 9a   **Fig. 9b**

 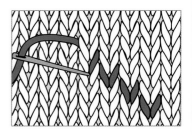

WEAVING SEAMS

With **right** side(s) facing and edges even, sew through both pieces once to secure the beginning of the seam, leaving an ample yarn end to weave in later. Insert the needle under the bar **between** the first and second stitches on the row and pull the yarn through *(Fig. 10)*. Insert the needle under the next bar on the second side. Repeat from side to side, being careful to match rows. If the edges are different lengths, it may be necessary to insert the needle under two bars at one edge.

Fig. 10

EMBROIDERY STITCHES
BACKSTITCH

The backstitch is worked from **right** to **left**. Come up at 1, go down at 2 and come up at 3 *(Fig. 11)*. The second stitch is made by going down at 1 and coming up at 4.

Fig. 11

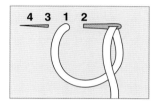

STRAIGHT STITCH

Straight stitch is just what the name implies, a single, straight stitch. Come up at 1 and go down at 2 *(Fig. 12)*.

Fig. 12

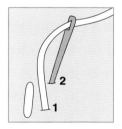

FRENCH KNOT

Bring the needle up at 1. Wrap the yarn around the needle 5 times and insert the needle at 2, holding the end of yarn with the nonstitching fingers *(Fig. 13)*. Tighten the knot; then pull the needle through, holding the yarn until it must be released.

Fig. 13

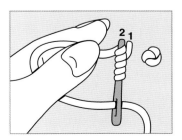

BASIC CROCHET STITCHES

JOINING WITH A SLIP STITCH

When instructed to join with a slip stitch, begin with a slip knot on the hook. Insert the hook in the stitch indicated, YO and draw through stitch **and** through loop on hook *(Fig. 14)*.

Fig. 14

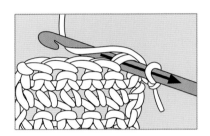

CHAIN *(abbreviated ch)*

To work a chain stitch, begin with a slip knot on the hook. Bring the yarn **over** the hook from **back** to **front**, catching the yarn with the hook and turning the hook slightly toward you to keep the yarn from slipping off. Draw the yarn through the stitch on the hook *(Fig. 15)* (**first chain st made**).

Fig. 15

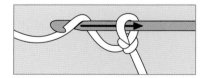

BACK RIDGE

Work in loops indicated by arrows *(Fig. 16)*.

Fig. 16

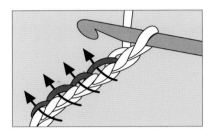

SLIP STITCH *(abbreviated slip st)*

To work a slip stitch, insert hook in stitch indicated, YO and draw through stitch and through loop on hook *(Fig. 17)* (**slip stitch made**).

Fig. 17

FINISH OFF

When you complete your last stitch, cut the yarn leaving a 4-6" (10-15 cm) end. Bring the loose end through the last loop on your hook and tighten it *(Fig. 18)*.

Fig. 18

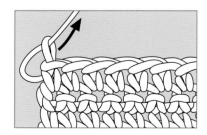

YARN INFORMATION

The Hats in this book were made using a Medium Weight or a Bulky Weight Yarn. Any brand of Medium Weight or Bulky Weight Yarn may be used. It is best to refer to the yardage/meters when determining how many balls or skeins to purchase. Remember, to achieve the same look, it is the weight of yarn that is important, not the brand of yarn.

For your convenience, listed below are the specific yarns used to create our photography models.

FOOTBALL HAT
Bernat® Handicrafter Cotton
Brown - #13130 Warm Brown
White - #00001 White

BASEBALL HAT
Bernat® Handicrafter Cotton
White - #00001 White
Red - #13530 Country Red

BASKETBALL HAT
Red Heart® Soft® Yarn
Brown - #1882 Toast
Black - #4614 Black

CHRISTMAS HAT
Lion Brand® Vanna's Choice®
Red - #113 Scarlet
Lion Brand® Fun Fur®
White - #100 White

EASTER HAT
Red Heart® Soft Baby Steps®
Purple - #9590 Lavender
Pink - #9700 Baby Pink
Blue - #9800 Baby Blue
Yellow - #9200 Baby Yellow
Variegated - #9930 Binky Print

ST. PATRICK'S DAY HAT
Patons® Canadiana
Green - #10230 Cherished Green
Dk Green - #10237 Dark Green Tea

HEART HAT
Lion Brand® Cotton-Ease®
White - #100 Snow
Red - #113 Cherry

GHOST HAT
Bernat® Handicrafter Cotton
White - #00001 White
Lion Brand® Kitchen Cotton
Black - #153 Licorice

WITCH HAT
Red Heart® With Wool
Black - #0012 Jet
Orange - #0252 Tangerine

LEE ANN GARRETT

"My love for knitting small things and embellishing has led me to design these fun and different baby hats," Lee Ann Garrett says.

"My grandmother put my first set of knitting needles in my hands when I was just 10 years old. I designed and knit my own Barbie doll clothes using scraps of fur and sequins to decorate them."

She's been designing baby hats for 10 years now. "I started with a couple of fruit hats and it has grown into 40 original designs. I have turned it into a full-time business and sell my hats at local farmer's markets, craft shows, specialty boutiques, and on-line."

Mothers and grandmothers have fun making her whimsical baby hats, she says, and they are great for using in newborn pictures, as well as for learning to knit in the round.

To see more of Lee Ann's designs, visit her Farm Fresh Baby Hats shop on Etsy.com and her new website, homegrownhats.ca.

Lee Ann has been knitting and designing a variety of projects for more than 40 years. She also has had a lifelong passion in crafts, including decoupage, crocheting, cross stitch, decorative painting, and sewing.

The retired registered nurse lives with her husband and dog in Ontario, Canada. Other interests include playing guitar, singing in a choir, and outdoor sports such as skiing, skating, camping, and canoeing.

We have made every effort to ensure that these instructions are accurate and complete. We cannot, however, be responsible for human error, typographical mistakes, or variations in individual work.

Production Team: Instructional/Technical Editor - Lois J. Long; Editorial Writer - Susan Frantz Wiles; Senior Graphic Artist - Lora Puls; Graphic Artist - Becca Snider Tally; Photo Stylist - Christy Myers; and Photographers - Mark Mathews and Ken West.

Instructions tested and photo models made by Raymelle Greening.